The Four Orchestral Suites

BWV 1066–1069

From the Bach-Gesellschaft Edition

Johann Sebastian Bach

DOVER PUBLICATIONS, INC.
Mineola, New York

Bibliographical Note

This Dover edition, first published in 2000, is a republication of the four *Ouverturen* [Suites] in Volume 31, Part 1, "Orchesterwerke," edited by Alfred Dörffel, from *Johann Sebastian Bach's Werke*, originally published by the Bach-Gesellschaft, Breitkopf & Härtel, Leipzig, 1885. Newly added are lists of contents and instrumentation, as well as score eye-guides to facilitate reading.

International Standard Book Number: 0-486-40863-9

Manufactured in the United States of America
Dover Publications, Inc., 31 East 2nd Street, Mineola, N.Y. 11501

CONTENTS

Bach referred to this set of orchestral suites as "Ouverturen," which strictly applies only to the first movement of each work, cast in the three-part form of a "French overture" but unnamed in the manuscript. The order of the suites appears to be chronological: Nos. 1 and 2 are from the Cöthen period, ca. 1721; Nos. 3 and 4 are probably from the years 1729 to 1736 in the Leipzig period. • BWV numbers refer to Wolfgang Schmieder's *Bach-Werke-Verzeichnis* [Catalog of Bach's Works], the standard systematic-thematic reference work for the music of Johann Sebastian Bach.

THE FOUR ORCHESTRAL SUITES

Orchestral Suite No. 1 in C Major

BWV 1066 / *ca.* 1721

[Ouverture] • Courante
Gavottes I, II • Forlane • Menuets I, II
Bourrées I, II • Passepieds I, II

INSTRUMENTATION

2 Oboes
Bassoon [Fagotto]

Violins I, II [Violino]
Violas
Continuo

Courante.

Gavotte I. alternativement.

Gavotte II.

Forlane.

Gavotte I. da Capo.

Menuet I. alternativement.

Menuet II.

Bourrée I. alternativement.

Bourrée II.

Bourrée I. da Capo.

Passepied I.

Passepied II.

piano

Passepied I. da Capo.

Orchestral Suite No. 2 in B Minor

BWV 1067 / *ca.* 1721

[Ouverture] • Rondeau
Sarabande • Bourrées I, II
Polonaise • Menuet • Badinerie

INSTRUMENTATION

Flute [Flauto traverso]

Violins I, II [Violino]
Violas
Continuo

Lentement.

tasto solo

Rondeau.

Sarabande.

Bourrée I.

Bourrée II.

Bourrée I.
da Capo.

Polonaise.
Moderato e staccato.

Double.

Polonaise
da Capo.

Menuet.

Badinerie.

staccato

Orchestral Suite No. 3 in D Major

BWV 1068 / *ca.* 1729–36

[Ouverture] • Air • Gavottes I, II
Bourrée • Gigue

INSTRUMENTATION

3 Trumpets [Tromba]
Timpani
2 Oboes

Violins I, II [Violino]
Violas
Continuo

Tromba I.

Tromba II.

Tromba III.

Timpani.

Oboe I.

Oboe II.

Violino I.

Violino II.

Viola.

Continuo.

45

Air.

Violino I.

Violino II.

Viola.

Continuo.

Gavotte I.

Gavotte II.

Gavotte I. da Capo.

Bourrée.

Gigue.

Orchestral Suite No. 4 in D Major

BWV 1069 / *ca.* 1729–36

[Ouverture] • Bourrées I, II
Gavotte • Menuets I, II • Réjouissance

INSTRUMENTATION

3 Trumpets [Tromba]
Timpani
3 Oboes
Bassoon [Fagotto]

Violins I, II [Violino]
Violas
Continuo

73

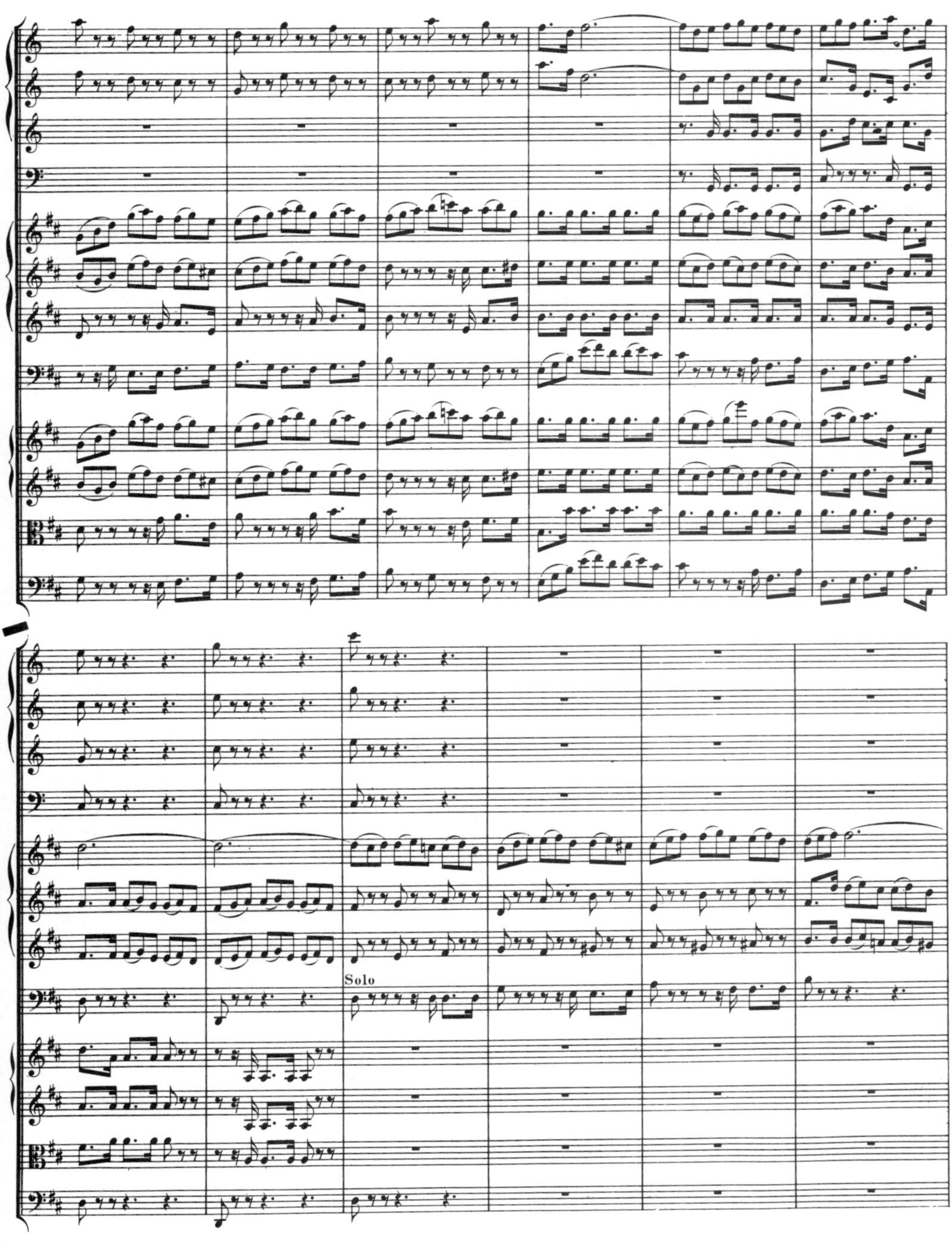
Solo

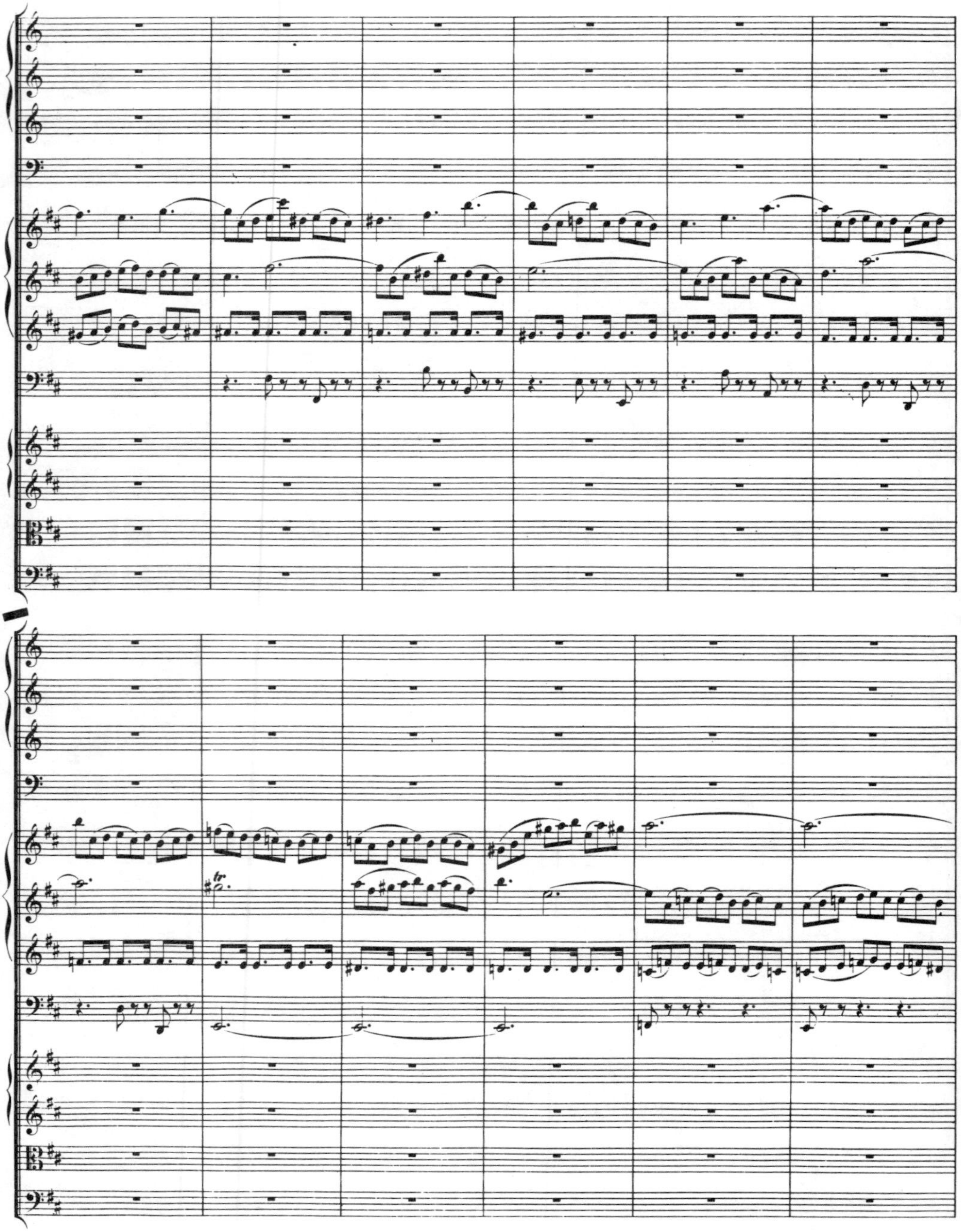

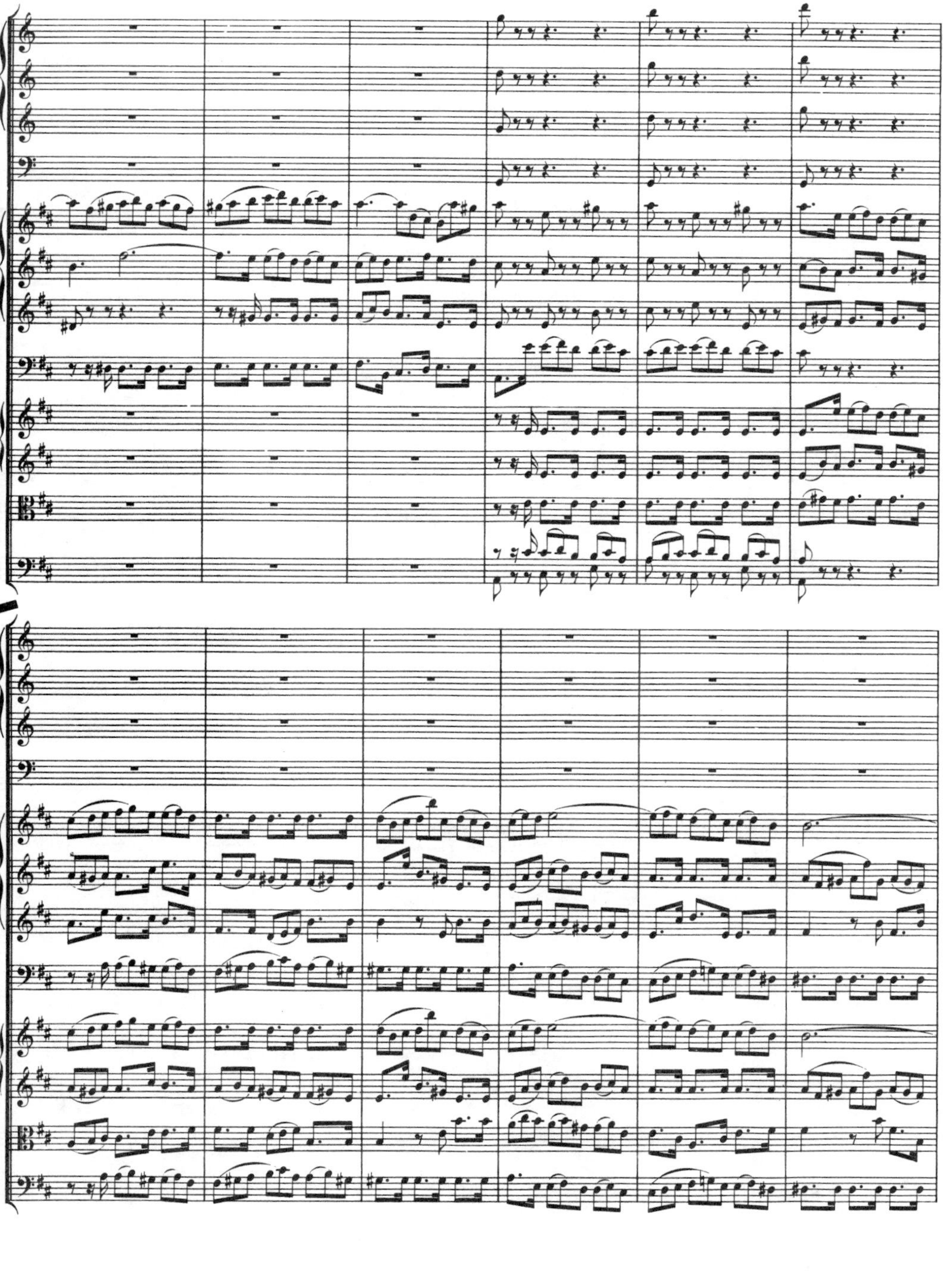

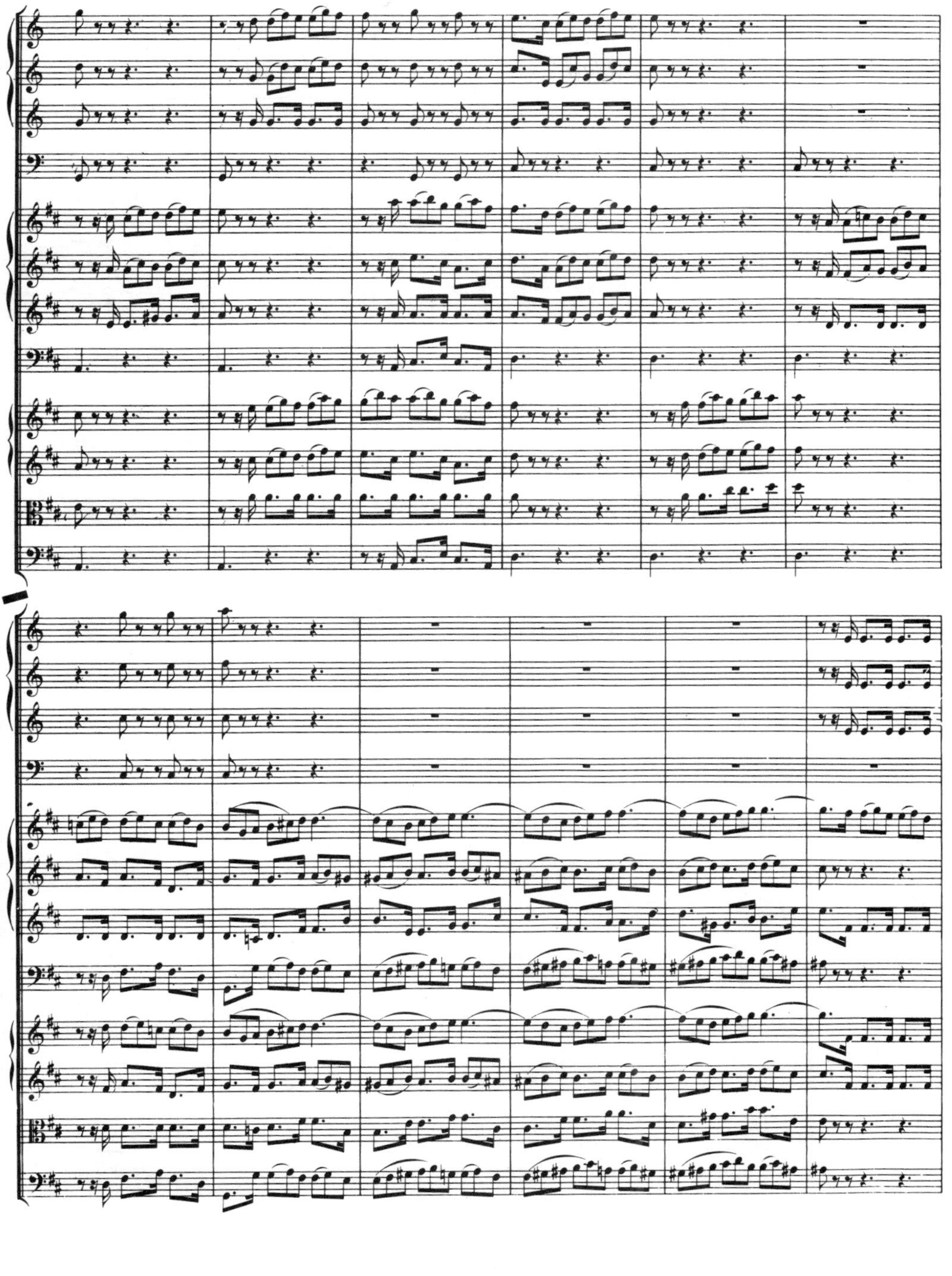

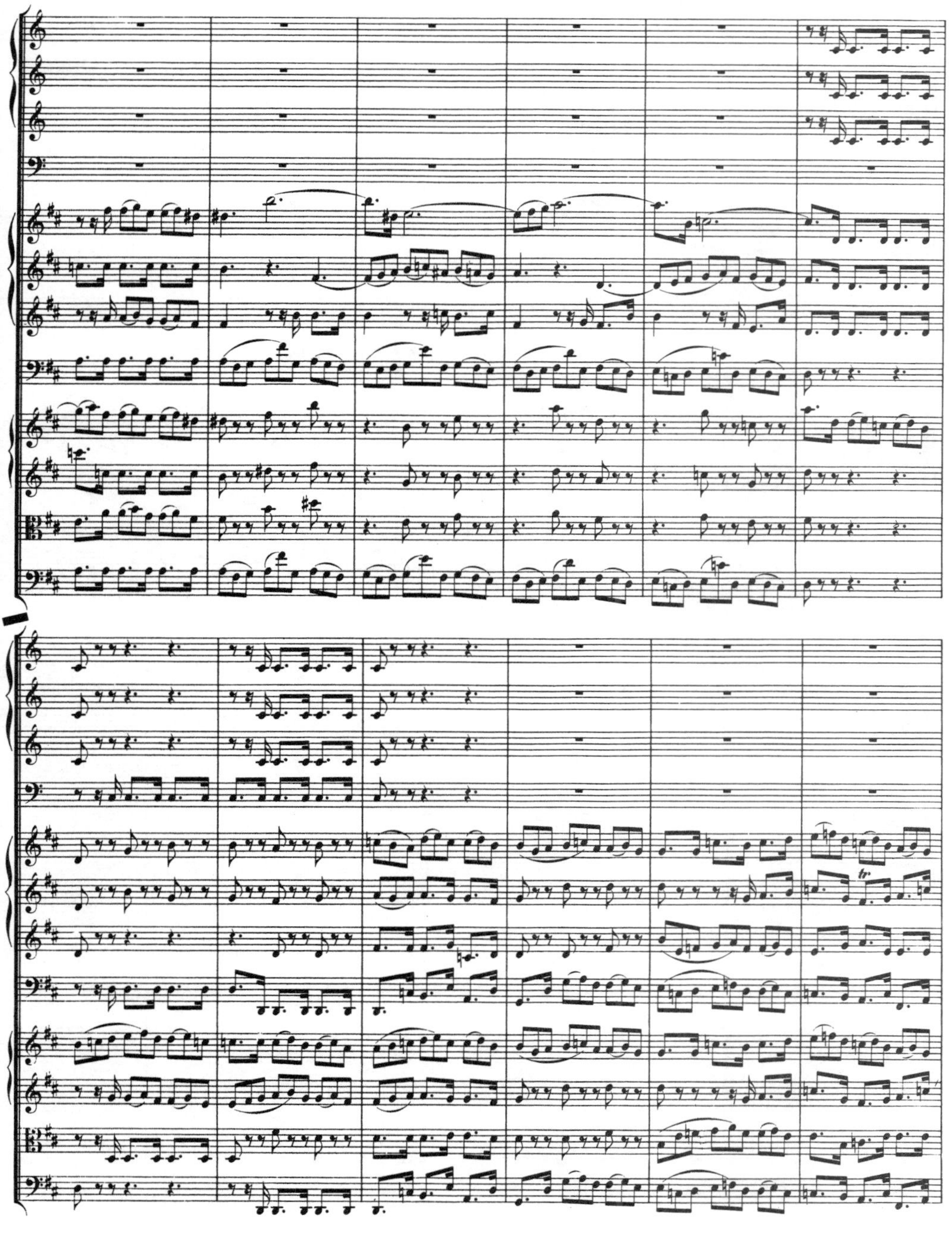
tr

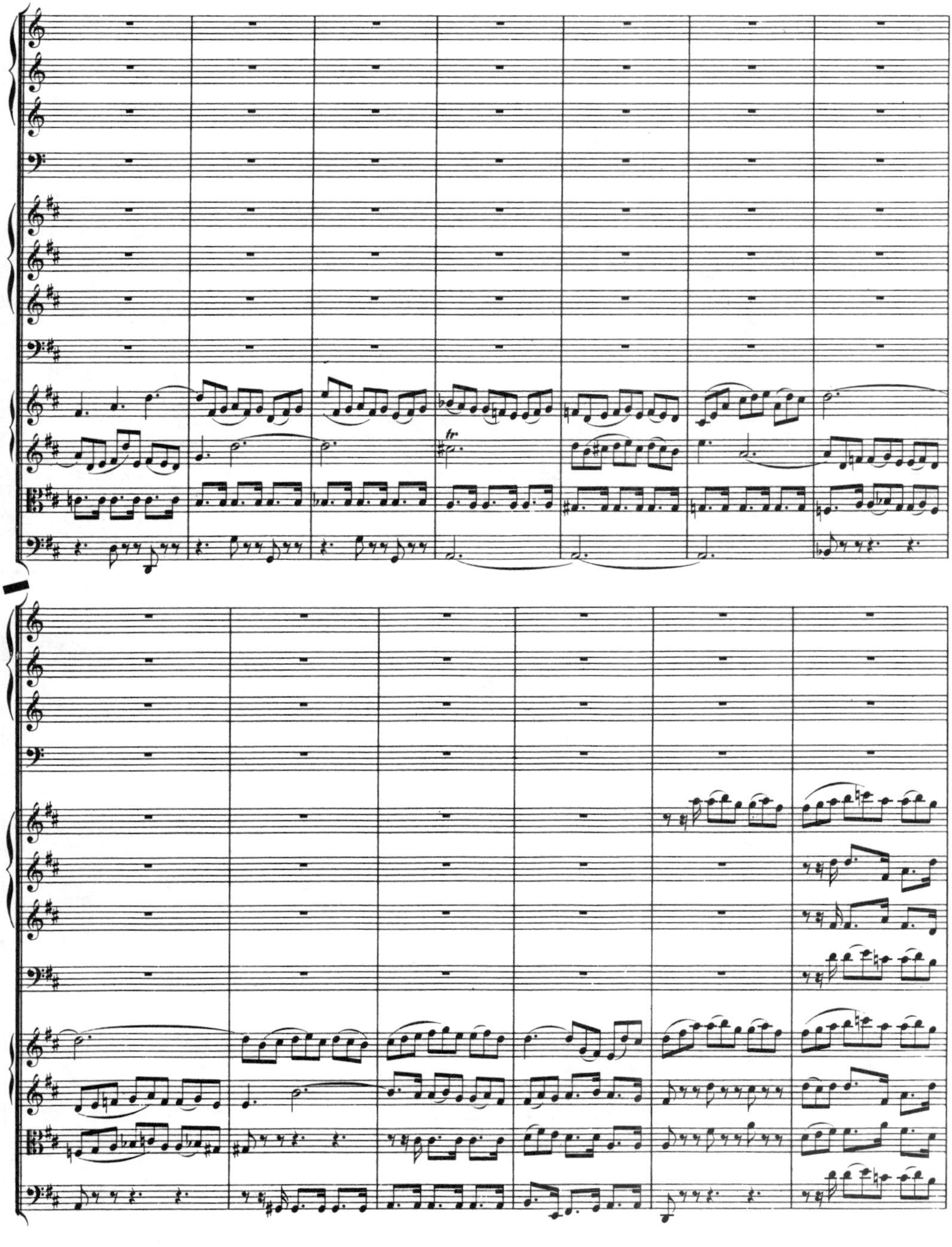

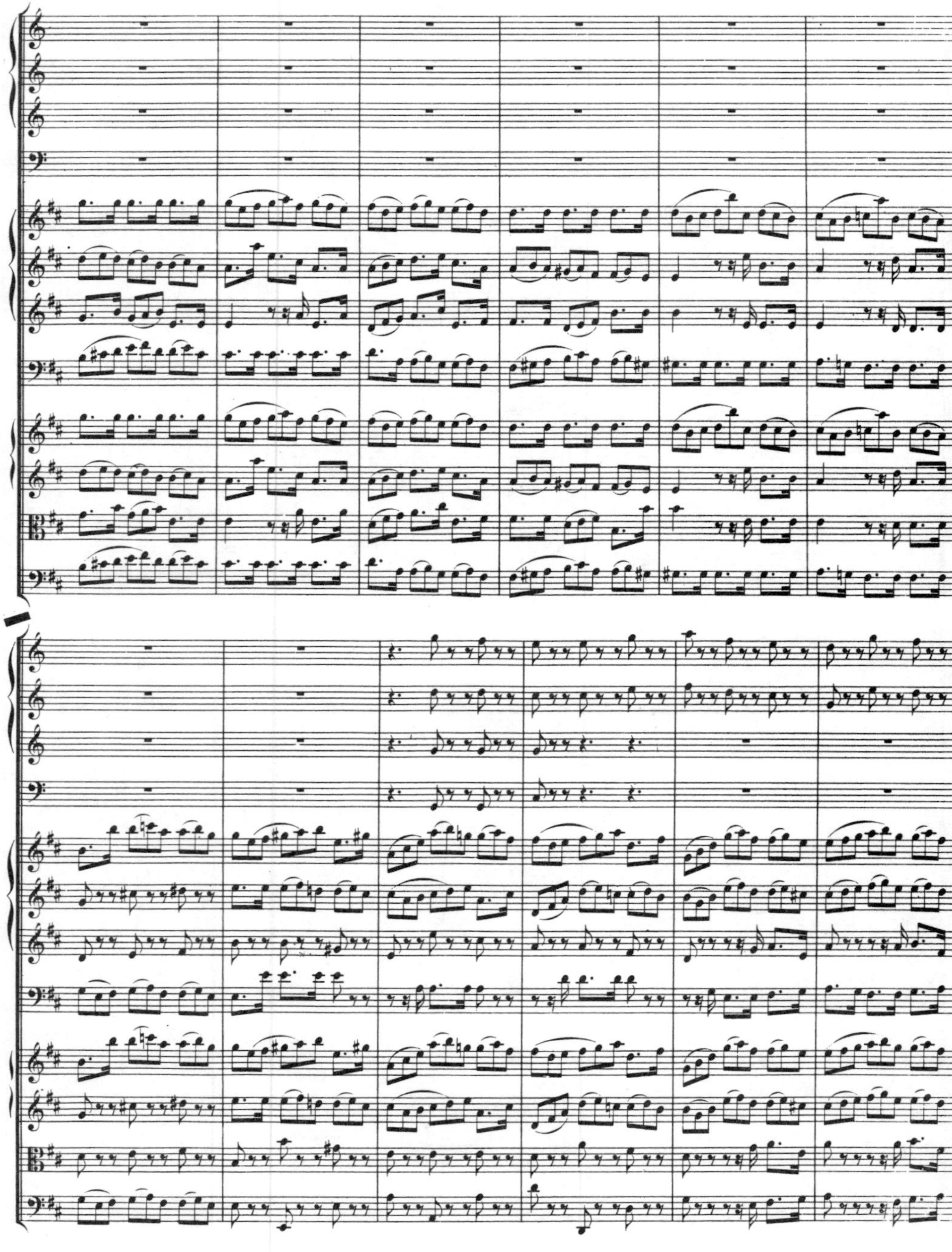

Bourrée I.

Bourrée II.

Bourrée I. da Capo.

Gavotte.

Menuet I.
alternativement.

Menuet II.

Réjouissance.

Menuet I. da Capo.

END OF EDITION

DOVER FULL-SIZE ORCHESTRAL SCORES

THE SIX BRANDENBURG CONCERTOS AND THE FOUR ORCHES-TRAL SUITES IN FULL SCORE, Johann Sebastian Bach. Complete standard Bach-Gesellschaft editions in large, clear format. Study score. 273pp. 9 x 12.   23376-6 Pa. **$12.95**

COMPLETE CONCERTI FOR SOLO KEYBOARD AND ORCHESTRA IN FULL SCORE, Johann Sebastian Bach. Bach's seven complete concerti for solo keyboard and orchestra in full score from the authoritative Bach-Gesellschaft edition. 206pp. 9 x 12.
24929-8 Pa. **$11.95**

THE THREE VIOLIN CONCERTI IN FULL SCORE, Johann Sebastian Bach. concerto in A Minor, BWV 1041; Concerto in E Major, BWV 1042; and Concerto for Two Violins in D Minor, BWV 1043. Bach-Gesellschaft edition. 64pp. 9⅜ x 12¼.
25124-1 Pa. **$6.95**

GREAT ORGAN CONCERTI, OPP. 4 & 7, IN FULL SCORE, George Frideric Handel. 12 organ concerti composed by great Baroque master are reproduced in full score from the *Deutsche Handelgesellschaft* edition. 138pp. 9⅜ x 12¼.   24462-8 Pa. **$12.95**

COMPLETE CONCERTI GROSSI IN FULL SCORE, George Frideric Handel. Monumental Opus 6 Concerti Grossi, Opus 3 and "Alexander's Feast" Concerti Grossi—19 in all—reproduced from most authoritative edition. 258pp. 9⅜ x 12¼.   24187-4 Pa. **$13.95**

LATER SYMPHONIES, Wolfgang A. Mozart. Full orchestral scores to last symphonies (Nos. 35–41) reproduced from definitive Breitkopf & Härtel Complete Works edition. Study score. 285pp. 9 x 12.   23052-X Pa. **$14.95**

PIANO CONCERTOS NOS. 17–22, Wolfgang Amadeus Mozart. Six complete piano concertos in full score, with Mozart's own cadenzas for Nos. 17–19. Breitkopf & Härtel edition. Study score. 370pp. 9⅜ x 12¼.   23599-8 Pa. **$16.95**

PIANO CONCERTOS NOS. 23–27, Wolfgang Amadeus Mozart. Mozart's last five piano concertos in full score, plus cadenzas for Nos. 23 and 27, and the Concert Rondo in D Major, K.382. Breitkopf & Härtel edition. Study score. 310pp. 9⅜ x 12¼.
23600-5 Pa. **$16.95**

DAPHNIS AND CHLOE IN FULL SCORE, Maurice Ravel. Definitive full-score edition of Ravel's rich musical settings of a Greek fable by Longus is reprinted here from the original French edition. 320pp. 9⅜ x 12¼. (Not available in France or Germany) 25826-2 Pa. **$17.95**

THREE GREAT ORCHESTRAL WORKS IN FULL SCORE, Claude Debussy. Three favorites by influential modernist: *Prélude à l'Après-midi d'un Faune, Nocturnes,* and *La Mer.* Reprinted from early French editions. 279pp. 9 x 12.   24441-5 Pa. **$14.95**

SYMPHONY IN D MINOR IN FULL SCORE, César Franck. Superb, authoritative edition of Franck's only symphony, an often-performed and recorded masterwork of late French romantic style. 160pp. 9 x 12.   25373-2 Pa. **$11.95**

THE GREAT WALTZES IN FULL SCORE, Johann Strauss, Jr. Complete scores of eight melodic masterpieces: The Beautiful Blue Danube, Emperor Waltz, Tales of the Vienna Woods, Wiener Blut, four more. Authoritative editions. 336pp. 8⅜ x 11¼.
                                                        26009-7 Pa. **$14.95**

THE FIREBIRD IN FULL SCORE (Original 1910 Version), Igor Stravinsky. Handsome, inexpensive edition of modern masterpiece, renowned for brilliant orchestration, glowing color. Authoritative Russian edition. 176pp. 9⅜ x 12¼. (Available in U.S. only)
                                                        25535-2 Pa. **$10.95**

PETRUSHKA IN FULL SCORE: Original Version, Igor Stravinsky. The definitive full-score edition of Stravinsky's masterful score for the great Ballets Russes 1911 production of *Petrushka.* 160pp. 9⅜ x 12¼. (Available in U.S. only)   25680-4 Pa. **$11.95**
